HOLT

Civic
Participation
Activities Guide

HOLT, RINEHART AND WINSTON

A Harcourt Education Company

Orlando • **Austin** • New York • San Diego • Toronto • London

ISBN 0-03-041919-0

9 10 11 12 13 14 15   0956   12 11 10 09

To the Teacher

This Civic Participation Activities Guide workbook provides students with activities that explore the nature of citizenship in the United States. Particular focus is placed on active citizen involvement in various areas of public affairs and government.

Each lesson includes a Teacher's Guide to help you teach the activity. Each lesson also includes any student handouts necessary to support the lesson. The lessons include an activity that provides active student participation. Activities include simulations, mock trials, community service projects, opportunities for civic participation, group and individual projects and presentations, writing letters, conducting polls or surveys, and conducting interviews. Several sources, such as California's civic values and democratic understanding curriculum strand, have been used as examples on which to base these activities.

Civic Participation Activities Guide

Contents

OVERVIEW

Students will learn the importance of government and laws in their daily lives as they examine the consequences of the absence of laws. Students will work together to create a classroom constitution that represents the values of the class as a whole and can be used throughout the school year.

PLANNING

Time Suggested

Two 45-minute class periods

Materials

- Student Handout 1: Governments and Constitutions
- Copies of the United States Constitution (located in student textbook)
- Student Handout 2: Writing a Classroom Constitution
- Butcher paper and markers

Group Size

Organize students into groups of 3 to 5 students each.

OBJECTIVES

- Students will understand the role of law in society.
- Students will examine the organization and elements of the U.S. Constitution.
- Students will play an active role in determining guidelines for classroom conduct.
- Students will participate in the political process by engaging in debate, learning to compromise, and ratifying their classroom guidelines.

PROCEDURE

1. **Focus Activity** Write these labels on the board: Shopping at a Mall; Driving on Streets and Highways; Attending a Football Game; and Sitting in Your Home. Ask students to think about laws and rules that are followed in each of these cases. To stimulate discussion, ask questions such as, "Can you take anything you want from a store at the mall?" "Could someone keep you from attending the game because of the color of your hair?" "Can your neighbors play loud music outside your window all night?" Each group should discuss the laws that are followed in various places. Then they should discuss what life would be like with no laws. Help students understand that the absence of laws often results in disorder and that a government makes laws and keeps order.

2. Distribute copies of **Student Handout 1: Governments and Constitutions.** Have student groups discuss and debate the questions in *Part One: The Nature of Government.* Groups should come to a consensus on their answers to these questions. When groups have completed the questions, engage the class in a discussion of their answers. Answers to Part

One is in the answer key. Be sure to help students understand the importance of governments and constitutions in establishing law and order.

3. Next explain that students will be creating a classroom constitution. Have each group review the U.S. Constitution (available in the student textbook). Explain that the Constitution states the basic laws of the United States government. Ask students to locate the preamble, the articles, and the amendments. Ask students to look through the Constitution to answer the questions in *Part Two: The Constitution.* After students answer the questions, lead a class discussion of the answers. Answers to Part Two are in the answer key.

4. Distribute copies of **Student Handout 2: A Classroom Constitution.** Explain that the class will write a classroom constitution that the class will follow for the remainder of the year. Start with a preamble. Ask groups to identify the elements that make up the preamble of the U.S. Constitution. Help students see that the preamble establishes the purpose of the Constitution ("to establish justice, insure domestic Tranquility, provide for the common defence"). Have each group write a rough draft of a preamble for the classroom constitution. Call on each group to share their ideas as you write them for the class to see. Using the list of ideas, help the class reach consensus on a final version of their preamble. Students can debate points they feel strongly about. Ask a student to write the final draft on a large piece of butcher paper.

5. Repeat the process to have each group write rules to be included in a classroom constitution. Each group should review the bulleted items on the handout and develop a set of three to four rules. If students need help getting started, state the following rule (or one of your own) as an example: "All students have the right to a peaceful and supportive learning environment." Ask each group to present their proposed rules to the class. After all groups have presented, lead the class in a discussion of each proposed rule. Encourage the students to seek compromise if there are rules on which they cannot agree. Finally conduct a class vote to "ratify" the constitution. A two-thirds majority can be used to accept the constitution. Have students write the final draft on butcher paper for all to see. Students may even sign the constitution they created.

ENRICHMENT

Have students call the mayor's office in your town and ask how local laws are made. Encourage students to interview local lawmakers to find out what laws are currently under consideration. Conduct a class discussion of the pros and cons of these laws.

Name _____ Class _____ Date _____

Governments and Constitutions   Civic Participation

PART ONE: THE NATURE OF GOVERNMENT

Discuss each of the following questions as a group and come to an
answer agreeable to all.

1. Why is government necessary?

_____

2. What responsibilities does a government have to its citizens?

_____

_____

3. What responsibilities do citizens have to their government?

_____

_____

4. Why are laws important?

_____

_____

5. What problems might arise if a government had no constitution?

_____

_____

PART TWO: THE CONSTITUTION

As your group examines the U.S. Constitution, answer the following
questions.

6. What are some of the topics of the seven articles of the Constitution?

_____

_____

7. What is the Bill of Rights? What is the purpose of the Bill of Rights?

_____

_____

8. What basic rights are granted to citizens in the Bill of Rights?

_____

_____

Name _____ Class _____ Date _____

Writing a Classroom Constitution   Civic Participation

Today you and your classmates will help your teacher create a classroom constitution. It should help guide the students' and teacher's conduct and expectations in the classroom.

The Preamble Many constitutions begin with a brief preamble, or introduction, that states the purpose and goals of the document. Use the following preamble as a model of what to include in your own preamble.

> **We the People of the United States, in Order to form a more perfect Union, establish Justice, insure domestic Tranquility, provide for the common defence, promote the general Welfare, and secure the Blessings of Liberty to ourselves and our Posterity, do ordain and establish this Constitution for the United States of America.**
>
> **–Preamble to the United States Constitution**

With your group, develop a preamble to your classroom constitution. Be sure to include major goals you hope to promote in the constitution.

We, the Students of _____

_____

_____

The Constitution Your classroom constitution will be made up of "laws" to promote order so that your class functions smoothly. With your group, develop a list of three or four rules that you would like to see included in the classroom constitution. Be sure to consider the following when creating your list:

- rights and responsibilities of students
- rights and responsibilities of teacher
- how rights and responsibilities will be enforced
- rules for maintaining order among students

_____

_____

_____

_____

Civic Participation

OVERVIEW

Students will learn that in American democracy, citizens have rights based on such civic values as honesty, liberty, fairness, safety, privacy, and equality. But for society to be successful, citizens must also assume duties and responsibilities. Students will discuss some of these rights and responsibilities. They will work together to make decisions in situations where rights and responsibilities may conflict with each other.

PLANNING

Time Suggested

Two 45-minute class periods

Materials

- Stopwatch
- Student Handout 1: Rights, Duties, and Responsibilities
- Student Handout 2: Deciding Among Rights and Responsibilities

Group Size

Organize students into groups of 3 to 5 students each.

OBJECTIVES

- Students will understand the civic values that underlie American democracy, including liberty, privacy, fairness, safety, and equality.
- Students will understand the role of citizens in American democracy.
- Students will distinguish between the responsibilities, duties, and rights of citizens.
- Students will decide among competing rights and responsibilities.

PROCEDURE

1. **Focus Activity** Look around the class and make note of students who are wearing glasses (or are wearing red clothing, or are taller than average, or are sitting in a certain row). Announce to students that during their next lunch period, certain students must stay in class and skip lunch (if this is permissible—if not, you can have the designated students stand for five minutes or you can call on only those students for answers). Name those people wearing glasses (or red clothing, or who are taller, or who are sitting in the secret row). Students will probably question and complain about this policy. Discuss those complaints with the class. Ask students to explain what they think is wrong. Ask student if they can guess why this group of students was singled out. When the class has guessed what those students have in common, lead a discussion about why this policy is unfair. Ask students if they think that your policy violated one of their rights. Encourage them to say that all students were not treated fairly or equally.

2. Discuss the fact that citizens have rights that deal with liberty, such as freedom of speech and religion. Citizens have these rights equally, regardless of age, gender, race, religion, or political beliefs. Citizens have similar rights that deal with safety, privacy, and security, such

as the rights that protect them from being arrested, searched, or punished without good reason. Discuss with students what they think that the role of government should be in relation to these rights. Ask students if they think that the government is fulfilling that role today. Also discuss with students what responsibilities they think that citizens have to ensure and protect their rights. Ask them what they think might happen if citizens had rights but no responsibilities.

3. Ask each group of students to write down as many responsibilities of citizens they can think of in 60 seconds. Time the activity. After 60 seconds, ask a representative of each group to read the responsibilities. Discuss any differences in the responses.

4. Distribute **Student Handout 1: Rights, Duties, and Responsibilities.** Ask students to explain the difference between duties and responsibilities. Help them understand that duties are things that are required from citizens. Responsibilities are things citizens should do for our government to work well. Ask each group to put the items from the left column into the three boxes on the right. When the groups have completed this task, discuss the answers. If there is disagreement, have students explain their decisions. Answers to Student Handout 1 are in the answer key.

5. Distribute copies of **Student Handout 2: Whose Rights and Responsibilities?** Help students understand that sometimes one person's rights or responsibilities conflicts with another person's rights or responsibilities. For example, the right to free speech is not unlimited: a person cannot stand up in a crowded theater and shout "Fire" if there is not a fire. Discuss with students why shouting "fire" in a crowded theater might violate other people's rights. It is not always easy to decide the best way to resolve a conflict between rights or responsibilities. Have the groups of students answer the questions on the handout. Remind students that if they don't agree, they should talk about their reasons and try to persuade the others. When the handouts are complete, have the groups compare their responses.

ENRICHMENT

1. Have students learn more about the 1954 Supreme Court case of *Brown* v. *Board of Education*. Ask them to report on the arguments made by each side in the case. Ask what rights Oliver Brown and the Topeka Board of Education were fighting for. Ask how the Supreme Court interpreted the Fourteenth Amendment's guarantee of equal protection of the laws in this case.

2. Have students pick a topic that deals with individual rights, such as affirmative action, privacy, or the military draft for females. Have students prepare a speech that takes a stand on one of these issues.

Rights, Duties, and Responsibilities

Civic Participation

Write the items in the left column into the appropriate boxes on the right.

Pay taxes to support police department, fire department, schools, and roads.	**RIGHTS**
Be informed about government issues.	
Attend school.	
Write an article criticizing the president.	
Serve on a jury.	
Vote in elections.	
Keep others out of your house.	**RESPONSIBILITIES**
Obey traffic laws.	
Have a lawyer with you if you are arrested.	
Volunteer to keep the environment clean.	
Buy a home in any neighborhood you like.	
Respect other people's property.	**DUTIES**
Register for the military draft (men 18 years and older).	

Name _____ Class _____ Date _____

Whose Rights and Responsibilities? Citizenship Participation

A. Tom told you that he put his new camera down in the cafeteria and now it is missing. You think you saw Marsha with a new camera. Today you and your classmates will help your teacher create a constitution to guide conduct and expectations in your classroom.

   1. What are Tom's rights?

   _____

   2. What are Marsha's rights?

   _____

   3. What is your responsibility?

   _____

   4. What would you do?

   _____

B. The principal has announced a new rule: Students may no longer ride bikes to school because there is too much traffic around the school.

   5. What is the principal's responsibility?

   _____

   6. What is the student's responsibility?

   _____

   7. What are the students' rights?

   _____

   8. Do you agree with the rule? If not, what would you do to try to change it?

   _____

C. Someone is giving a protest speech in front of City Hall. So many people are listening to the speech that traffic cannot pass on the street. The mayor must decide what to do.

   9. What is the speaker's right?

   _____

   10. What is the mayor's responsibility?

   _____

   11. What would you do if you were the mayor?

   _____

Civic Participation

OVERVIEW

This lesson will help students understand the variety of governments that exist around the world. Students will research the governments of different countries and analyze how each government affects the citizens of the country.

PLANNING

Time Suggested

Two to three 45-minute class periods

Materials

- Student Handout 1: Types of Government
- Student Handout 2: Comparing Governments

Group Size

Organize students into two large groups for the Focus Activity. The other activities require groups of 3 to 5 students each.

OBJECTIVES

- Students will research the definitions of different types of government and analyze the advantages and disadvantages of each.
- Students will research the governments of six countries to compare the roles of leaders and citizens.
- Students will predict how citizens in different countries might react to the same government policy, and write newspaper articles that show how different types of governments affect the reactions of citizens and the reporting of news.

SUGGESTED RESOURCES

Some helpful resources might include *The CIA World Factbook: 2004* (available on the Internet), *World Almanac and Book of Facts* (latest edition), or recent encyclopedias or online databases that provide information on countries.

PROCEDURE

1. **Focus Activity** Begin by dividing the class into two large groups. Inform students that one group is a dictatorship and the other a democracy. Choose one student to rule as the dictator of his or her group, but do not put anyone in charge of the democratic group. Tell students that their task is to decide where their group will go for an imaginary class field trip. Allow the groups some time to determine their destination. The dictatorship group should quickly decide where they will go, and there will be little, if any, discussion. The democratic group, on the other hand, should have discussion and debate about where to go. After a few minutes, ask students in each group to reflect on the process. Did anyone feel left out of the decision-making process? Which process was easier? Why? Who had a say in each group? Help students see that although the democratic process is more time consuming, it allows citizens to express their opinions and play an active role in decision making.

2. Distribute **Student Handout 1: Types of Governments.** Organize students into three to five groups. Have groups of students use dictionaries, encyclopedias, or Internet sources to write definitions for the words listed in the first column. See Suggested Resources for more information. Then ask students to discuss the advantages and disadvantages of each type of government and to fill in the other columns. Answers to Part One are in the answer key. Be sure to help students understand the importance of governments and constitutions in establishing law and order.

3. Help students understand the similarities and differences between the different types of governments. Ask the following questions about types of government: Which types of government are more likely to control newspapers and television stations? (dictatorship, communist state) Which are more likely to let citizens vote on changes that will affect their communities? (democracy, republic) Which is more likely to have the leader gain his power by heredity? (monarchy)

4. After a discussion of Part One, have students individually answer the questions in Part Two. Ask students to read their answers and discuss any disagreements.

5. Distribute copies of **Student Handout 2: Comparing Governments.** Ask groups of students to research each of the countries and answer the questions in Part One. Be sure there is at least one group of students researching each country. After research is completed, read each question and have one student from each group answer it. Discuss how the countries are alike and different. Students may discover such terms as "constitutional monarchy" (Great Britain) and "federal republic" (United States). Talk about the meanings of these terms.

6. Review the instructions for Part Two. Have the groups of students talk about how their country might react to a leader's decision to move the capital city. After the discussion, ask each student to write a short newspaper article. They should keep in mind who controls the news media in their country and what rights citizens have to express their views.

ENRICHMENT

1. Have students research information to compare the government of Poland as a communist country starting in the mid-1940s and as a republic after 1989.

2. Have students write biographies about a dictator, such as Adolf Hitler, Saddam Hussein, Fidel Castro, or Augusto Pinochet.

3. Encourage students to create a list of their daily activities for one day. Beside each activity, they should record how the activity might be different if they did not live in a federal republic, such as the United States.

Types of Government

Civic Participation

PART ONE: TYPES OF GOVERNMENT

Work with your group to research information to complete this chart.

Type of Government	Definition	Country	Advantages	Disadvantages
dictatorship				
republic				
monarchy				
democracy				
communism				

PART TWO: ANALYZING GOVERNMENTS

Answer the following questions on your own.

1. In which type of government do citizens have a greater influence on the laws that govern their lives?

_____

_____

2. Which type of government listed in the chart would you prefer? Why?

_____

_____

Comparing Governments   Civic Participation

PART ONE: RESEARCHING INFORMATION

With your group, choose one of these countries to research. Find
answers to these questions.

United States	Poland	Saudi Arabia
Cuba	Myanmar	Great Britain

1. What is the type of government?

_____

2. What is the name of the leader?

_____

3. How long has the leader been in office? Is there a law that limits the term?

_____

4. How is the leader chosen?

_____

5. Who makes the national laws?

_____

6. What rights do citizens have?

_____

PART TWO: WRITING A NEWS STORY

Think about how a newspaper in the country you chose would report
this event:

*The country's leader has decided to move the capital city. Homes and for-
ests must be demolished to make room for government buildings.*

Write the article including the announcement of the decision and the
reaction of the citizens.

OVERVIEW
Students will learn how to develop and refine their participatory skills as they examine the pros and cons of a community issue and write a letter to the editor of their local newspaper.

PLANNING
Time Suggested
Two 45-minute class periods

Materials
- Clippings of letters to the editor from a local newspaper
- Editorial guidelines for sending a letter to the editor, usually found on the editorial page
- Student Handout 1: Organizing an Interest Group
- Student Handout 2: Writing a Letter to the Editor

Preparation
- Collect information, such as newspapers articles, news footage, radio transcripts, and literature from the Web sites of interest groups, on an important issue that is being actively debated in the community.

Group Size
Organize students into two large groups.

OBJECTIVES
- Students will participate in activities that focus on a local issue.
- Students will learn methods and actions for influencing public opinion and government.
- Students will show a willingness to consider other points of view.
- Students will learn to write a persuasive letter that supports a local issue.

PROCEDURE
1. **Focus Activity** Begin by asking students to think of an instance when they tried to change something by themselves, acting alone. For example, have they tried to convince their classmates to play soccer instead of flag football after school? Did—or would—they have better luck if and when others joined their cause? Why? Point out that while one person can make a difference in many ways, people are more likely to be persuaded by a group than by an individual. Explain how actions of an organized group of people with a shared goal—commonly known as an *interest group*—can influence public opinion and advocate change in the government.

2. Next, ask students if they can give examples from history of how interest groups were instrumental in enacting change in the government. (Abolitionists fought for the end of slavery. Suffragists lobbied for women's rights to vote. Civil rights activists fought for equal rights regardless of race or color.) Then have students identify ways that an interest group might influence public opinion today. (Letter-writing campaigns to news media

or public officials, using the Internet to spread information, holding fundraisers to raise money to support the cause, and holding public demonstrations are just a few.) Identify interest groups that are widely known today, such as the American Civil Liberties Union (ACLU), National Rifle Association (NRA), National Wildlife Federation (NWF), American Association of Retired Persons (AARP), and National Association for the Advancement of Colored People (NAACP).

3. Organize the class into two groups. Ask students to identify a local issue that is actively being debated in the media. Ask them what they know about the issue. Help students identify the two sides to the issue by reading newspaper articles, talk radio transcripts, and literature from a local interest group's Web site, and by viewing local news footage. Students may want to find out if their local representative has made a statement on the issue.

4. Assign one group to advocate one side of the issue and the other group to represent the opposing side. Distribute copies of **Student Handout 1: Organizing an Interest Group.** Have students complete the handout. When they are finished, engage them in a discussion of the answers. Remind them of the power that an organized group can have in influencing community leaders' decisions. Then tell the students that each group will write a letter to the editor of the local newspaper supporting their side of the issue.

5. Distribute copies of **Student Handout 2: Writing a Letter to the Editor.** On the board, write a sample format for a business letter. Show the sender's name and address and the date in the upper right corner. Show the receiver's name and address on the left above the salutation. Have each group work together to draft, edit, and finalize a letter that calls for others to join them and support their cause. When both groups are finished, have each group read its letter aloud to the class. Ask students if an argument made by the opposing group would make them reconsider their point of view. Why? Then have each group mail its letter to the editor of the local newspaper. Monitor the newspaper to see if the letters are published. (Note: Some newspapers also accept letters to the editor via e-mail. If you choose this option of delivery, let students know that the format of the letter should remain the same as prescribed in **Student Handout 2.**)

ENRICHMENT

1. Have students follow the local issue to its resolution by creating a classroom bulletin board. Ask them to monitor the local media and add new clippings as well as other information as the issue develops over time. You will especially want to note if one of the letters to the editor is published and/or prompts additional letters to the editor.

2. Have students write a persuasive letter on the issue to their local representative.

Organizing an Interest Group   Civic Participation

A. Getting Organized

1. Summarize the issue.

_____

_____

2. What is your group's opinion about the issue?

_____

_____

3. Name your interest group.

_____

_____

B. Influencing Others

1. List three reasons why others should support your cause.

Reason #1:

_____

_____

Reason #2:

_____

_____

Reason #3:

_____

_____

2. Identify one argument opposing your position.

_____

_____

_____

_____

Name _____ Class _____ Date _____

Writing a Letter to the Editor   Civic Participation

Today your interest group will write a letter to the editor of your local newspaper. The goal is to persuade other readers to agree with your point of view and to help advocate for the outcome you support. Use the following organizer and your completed Student Handout to help organize and write a persuasive letter. Type your final letter in a business letter format. At the bottom, type your group's name, and have each group member sign the letter.

Paragraph 1: Name the issue that you are writing about, and state your group's position on it.

_____

_____

Paragraph 2: State Reason #1 from your handout. Include facts to support your group's position.

_____

_____

Paragraph 3: State Reason #2 from your handout. Again, include supporting facts.

_____

_____

Paragraph 4: State Reason #3 from your handout with supporting information.

_____

_____

Paragraph 5: Acknowledge an opposing argument (from your handout) and state how you refute it.

_____

_____

Paragraph 6: Call others to action by requesting that they write letters to their government representatives.

_____

_____

OVERVIEW

The United States government is called a federal republic. Citizens elect representatives who make public policy and pass laws. In a republic and a democracy, citizens have the chance to find out which candidates agree with their ideas and to vote for these candidates. Citizens can also affect public policy by voting on issues through the referendum process. Students will learn that voting is both a right and responsibility. Part of that responsibility includes becoming well informed about candidates for office and about election issues.

PLANNING
Time Suggested

Two 45-minute class periods

Materials

- newspaper articles, political cartoons, and ads about political candidates and issues—These should include examples of both biased and unbiased information.
- Student Handout One: Recognizing Propaganda
- Student Handout Two: Classroom Referendum

Suggested Resources

Political cartoons can be found on Internet sites such as http://cagle.slate.msn.com/politicalcartoons.

Group Size

Organize students into groups of 3 to 5 students each.

OBJECTIVES

- Students will learn that citizens have a right to influence public policy by voting for candidates who represent their point of view. Students will also learn that people and groups can affect public policy by supporting or opposing measures placed on the ballot by referendum.
- Students will understand that citizens have a responsibility to vote and to become informed about issues before voting.
- Students will distinguish between propaganda and unbiased political information.
- Students will learn how citizens can register to vote, and students will vote in a classroom referendum.

PROCEDURE

1. **Focus Activity** Challenge the class to think about the right to vote by announcing that you may not vote in the next election. Give reasons for not voting, such as

   - "I think you need to register several weeks before voting, and I'm not sure I have registered."
   - "I don't really know what the candidates stand for."
   - "My one vote isn't going to make a difference."
   - "I don't care—it's not my job to run the country. Let someone else vote."

   Encourage students to refute each of your arguments. Help students reach the conclusion that citizens should appreciate their right to vote and should use it to help govern the country. Students should also come to realize that citizens have a responsibility to register to vote and become informed about the issues before voting.

2. Explain that the United States is a federal republic. Citizens can influence the policies that affect their lives by electing representatives who share and represent their interests and values. Ask students to name their state's senators and representatives to Congress. Then ask them to name their local representatives to state government. If students do not know this information, help them locate it on the Internet or by phoning their local government.

3. Ask students to think of ways they could be better informed about candidates and issues. Make a list on the board. It may include reading newspaper stories, watching television evening news, watching or attending candidate debates, listening to television and radio talk shows, and looking at advertisements.

4. Show students examples of political information including news stories and political cartoons. Help students see the difference between unbiased information and propaganda.

5. Distribute copies of **Student Handout 1: Recognizing Propaganda.** Help students understand that unbiased sources provide the best information for making a decision, and that it is important to recognize propaganda. Have students work in small groups to answer the questions on the handout. Answers are provided in the answer key.

6. Explain that another way for citizens to voice their opinions is through a referendum. This is a method by which citizens can vote to approve or reject a policy passed by a state or local government. Discuss a referendum that has been relevant in your students' community. Explain that the class will hold a referendum on a classroom issue. Distribute **Student Handout 2: Classroom Referendum.** Have students complete Part One: Voter Registration.

7. Before the election, create a referendum issue that is relevant to the students (a new class seating arrangement, a new classroom policy or schedule, or a project assignment). Have small groups of students discuss the issue and complete Part Two: Discussing the Issue. Conduct a debate between those students who support and those who oppose the referendum. Have students for each side design a flyer that they might circulate to persuade others to their side. On the day of the election, collect voter registration cards from students. Those who do not return a completed card cannot vote. Conduct the election. Close with a brief discussion of the benefits of voting: students have a chance to have their opinions heard, to be part of the process, and to be active participants in their government.

ENRICHMENT

1. Assign groups of students to learn about the constitutional amendments that affect voting rights. These include the Fifteenth, Nineteenth, Twenty-third, Twenty-fourth, and Twenty-sixth Amendments. Each group should collaborate to make a poster that advocates the passage of the amendment. Then they should present the poster and information to the class. Discuss why these rights are important enough to require constitutional amendments.

2. Have students find information on the Internet about voter turnout. One source is http://www.census.gov/population/www/socdemo/voting.html. Students should find one or two interesting facts, such as a comparison of voter turnout in two different years or a comparison of women and men voters. Students should make a graph and present it to the class.

Name _____ Class _____ Date _____

Recognizing Propaganda Civic Participation

Before an election, you will see many kinds of information about the candidates. Some information is unbiased. It is meant to inform but not to influence your decision. Other information is propaganda. It is meant to persuade you to vote a certain way. You can use both types of information in making your voting decision. But be aware that propaganda presents only one side.

1. Write P before the statements that describe propaganda.

_____ **a.** Two candidates debate the issue of tax reform on national television.

_____ **b.** A television ad says, "Carol Candidate doesn't care about senior citizens."

_____ **c.** A newspaper article reports that Carol Candidate spoke in favor of gun control at a local university.

_____ **d.** A movie star gives a speech in favor of Ronnie Repp at a political rally.

_____ **e.** A radio talk-show hosts says, "Ronnie Repp will bring peace and prosperity to this country."

2. Which issues should a candidate support in order to win your vote?

_____ preserving the environment

_____ building military power

_____ supporting more funding for schools

_____ building better security in this country

_____ lowering taxes

Others:

_____

3. If you were voting in the next election, how would you become informed?

_____

_____

4. Suppose you strongly support a candidate and want to convince others to do so. Draw an illustration of or describe one way to convince others. Assume anything is possible. Here are some ideas: circulate a flyer with a political cartoon or a list of reasons; get a famous person to come to your town to talk about the candidate.

Civic Participation

Name _____ Class _____ Date _____

Classroom Referendum

PART ONE: VOTER REGISTRATION

Soon you and your classmates will hold a referendum. A referendum is a special type of vote in which citizens decide whether their government should take a particular action. To be eligible to vote in the upcoming referendum, you MUST be registered to vote. Be sure to complete the voter registration form below and submit it to your teacher by the day of the election.

Classroom Voter Registration Card

USE BLUE OR BLACK INK - PLEASE PRINT CLEARLY

1
Last Name

First Name   Middle/Maiden Name   GENDER
○ Male
○ Female

2
RESIDENCE ADDRESS (Address where you live)
Number   Dir.   Street Name   Type   Apt/Place

City   State   Zip Code   County

3
MAILING ADDRESS (if different from the address where you live) or P.O. BOX
Number   Dir.   Street Name   Type   Suffix   Apt/Place

City   State   Zip Code   Telephone
( ) -

4 Date of Birth (Required)   Place of Birth (State or Country Only)   **5** Driver's License #

I have read and understand the contents on this form. I certify under penalty of perjury that the information on this form is true and correct.

X _____
Signature

Today's Date ___ / ___ / _____

PART TWO: DISCUSSING THE ISSUE

1. Write the words of the referendum that will appear on the voting ballot.

_____

_____

2. Write a reason to support the referendum.

_____

_____

3. Write a reason to oppose the referendum.

_____

_____

OVERVIEW

Students will learn that people can be U.S. citizens by birth or by naturalization. By studying the process of naturalization, students will gain an appreciation for the rights of citizenship. By studying the Oath of Allegiance taken by new citizens, students will gain an understanding of the importance of the naturalization process.

PLANNING

Time Suggested

Two 45-minute class periods

Materials

- reference books or a computer for research on the U.S. definition of citizenship
- student Handout 1: The Naturalization Process
- student Handout 2: Loyalty
- a dictionary

Suggested Resources

Web site for U.S. Citizenship and Immigration Services is http://uscis.gov/graphics/services/natz

Group Size

Organize students into groups of 4 or 5.

OBJECTIVES

- Students will learn that people can become citizens by birth or by a naturalization process.
- Students will understand that naturalization is a serious process that could take several years.
- Students will answer sample history and government questions that illustrate the information required in the naturalization exam.
- Students will become familiar with the Oath of Allegiance, and write it in their own words.

PROCEDURE

1. **Focus Activity** Begin by saying that the class has been talking about the rights and responsibilities of citizens. Ask students to tell what they think is important about being U.S. citizens. They may talk about the rights, freedoms, and protections of the U.S. government. Then ask, "Who is a citizen?" Let students brainstorm the criteria for being a U.S. citizen. If needed, ask questions to encourage discussion, such as, "Suppose parents move here from another country and buy a house—do they become U.S. citizens? Are their children U.S. citizens? Suppose a tourist from another country gives birth in the U.S.—is the child a U.S. citizen?"

2. Suggest that groups of students research the Web site of U.S. Citizenship and Immigration Services (www.uscis.gov/graphics/services/natz/citizen.htm) to find out how the law defines a citizen by birth. They should report information such as the following:

   The Fourteenth Amendment to the Constitution guarantees citizenship to almost anyone born in the United States. (This includes territories of the United States, such as Puerto Rico and Guam.) If a child's parents are citizens of another country, but the child is born here, the child is a U.S. citizen. (If a parent is an official representative of a foreign government living in the U.S., the child usually does not become a U.S. citizen.) If a child is born outside the U.S., but both parents are U.S. citizens, the child is a U.S. citizen.

3. Explain that people who come to the U.S. to live (immigrants) must apply to the U.S. government to settle here. Although millions of people apply, only a few hundred thousand gain permission. They are called lawful permanent residents. They may hold jobs, own property, and attend school. They must obey laws and pay taxes. They cannot vote or run for office. After five years of residence, they may apply for citizenship through the naturalization process.

4. Distribute **Student Handout 1: The Naturalization Process.** Have the students read Part One and discuss the answers to the questions. Talk about classes or training a person might need to become a citizen. Then have students complete Part Two individually. Encourage them to look up answers to questions they do not know. After all the blanks are filled in, students should consult with others in their group to be sure everyone has the correct answers. Answers to Part Two are in the answer key.

5. Distribute **Student Handout 2: Loyalty.** Call on various students to read each separate phrase of the Oath of Allegiance. Talk about what the words mean, and be sure students understand each phrase before continuing to the next. Students should use a dictionary to define unfamiliar words. After discussing the words of the oath, ask students to rewrite it in their own words.

ENRICHMENT

1. Have a "Citizenship Bee." Give each student 8-10 index cards. Students should write one question about U.S. history or government on each card. They should write the answers on the back of the cards. Students can get questions from their textbooks or find sample questions on a government website at http://uscis.gov/graphics/exec/natz/natztest.asp. Collect all the cards and start the bee. Ask one question to each student. (When a student misses a question, he/she must leave the game and become the "asker.") Play the game until only one person is left. If time is running short and students are not getting eliminated, have students write "very challenging" questions to ask the remaining students.

2. Have students interview someone who has become a naturalized citizen. Before the interview, students should write questions about the person's reasons for wanting to become a citizen, the application process, and how becoming a citizen has affected the person's life. Students should report on their interviews to the class.

The Naturalization Process   Civic Participation

PART ONE: REQUIREMENTS FOR CITIZENSHIP

Immigrants can become U.S. citizens by the naturalization process.
This process includes filing applications, attending an interview with an
immigration official, and passing exams.

Requirements for Citizenship

- be at least 18 years old
- have lived in the U.S. as a legal resident for at least five years
- be of good moral character and loyal to the U.S.
- show the ability to read, write, speak, and understand basic English
- pass a test of basic knowledge of U.S. history and government
- take an oath of allegiance to the United States

1. Which of these requirements might be most challenging? Why?

_____

_____

2. Do you think these requirements are stricter for naturalized citizens than for citizens by birth? Explain.

_____

_____

3. Why do you think naturalized citizens must show an understanding of history, government, and English?

_____

_____

PART TWO: A SAMPLE TEST

Here are some questions that might appear on the citizenship examination. If you don't know the answer, look it up in your history book or in an encyclopedia.

1. How many stars are on the flag?

_____

2. What do the stars on the flag mean?

_____

The Naturalization Process, *continued*   Civic Participation

3. What is the name of the president's official home?

_____

4. What country did we fight in the Revolutionary War?

_____

5. Who becomes the president of the U.S. if the president dies?

_____

6. Why are there 100 senators in the Senate?

_____

7. How many amendments have there been to the Constitution?

_____

8. Who was president during the Civil War?

_____

Loyalty   Civic Participation

Becoming a Citizen

After a person's application is approved and an immigration official
decides that the person is qualified to become a U.S. citizen, the person
joins a group of people in court to take an oath of loyalty to the United
States.

The Oath of Allegiance to the United States

I hereby declare, on oath, that I absolutely and entirely renounce and
abjure all allegiance and fidelity to any foreign prince, potentate, state,
or sovereignty of whom or which I have heretofore been a subject or
citizen; that I will support and defend the Constitution and laws of the
United States of America against all enemies, foreign and domestic;
that I will bear true faith and allegiance to the same; that I will bear
arms on behalf of the United States when required by law; that I will
perform noncombatant service in the Armed Forces of the United
States when required by the law; that I will perform work of national
importance under civilian direction when required by the law; and that
I take this obligation freely without any mental reservation or purpose
of evasion; so help me God. In acknowledgement whereof I have here-
unto affixed my signature.

   After you discuss each section of the oath with your classmates,
rewrite the Oath in your own words.

_____

_____

_____

_____

_____

_____

_____

_____

_____

_____

OVERVIEW

Civic values, such as trustworthiness, fairness, responsibility, and respect, are important to successful society. Students will discuss the meanings of these values in their lives and try to solve problems by applying these values.

PLANNING

Time Suggested

Two 45-minute class periods

Materials

- Student Handout 1: Words of Wisdom
- Student Handout 2: Making Decisions

Group Size

Organize students into five groups.

OBJECTIVES

- Students will discuss the meaning of civic values such as trustworthiness, fairness, responsibility, and respect.
- Students will create and role-play situations in which people do and do not portray civic values.
- Students will try to learn about each other in an effort to develop mutual respect.
- Students will think about how words of wisdom have meaning in their lives.
- Students will try to solve a problem by considering the advantages and disadvantages of two options and applying civic values.

PROCEDURE

1. **Focus Activity** Begin by asking students what it means that someone is trustworthy. They may come up with meanings such as, "You know the person will tell you the truth," or "You can count on that person to do what she/he promises." Ask, "What if I asked to borrow your calculator, but you didn't think I was trustworthy?" Ask, "What kinds of behavior would make you not trust someone?" Explain that good citizens are trustworthy, respectful, responsible, and fair. Sometimes people must make difficult decisions. If they keep these values in mind, it may be easier to make good decisions.

2. Organize the class into five groups. Assign each group one of these character labels: Friends, Teacher/Students, Parents/Children, Employer/Employees, Citizens/Community. Ask each group to create two role-playing skits. In the first skit, some characters are not trustworthy (i.e., not honest and reliable). In the second skit, the characters are trustworthy. After each skit, have the class discuss the importance of honesty and reliability.

3. Write the word "Respect" on the board. Ask students to tell what they think respect means. Answers may include "being polite and courteous" and "not judging someone by outer appearances." Explain that it is important to respect people who have different backgrounds and beliefs from our own. One way to develop respect is to learn about the things that make you different and things that make you alike. Pair students and ask each pair to talk to each other until they can list five ways that they are different and five ways that they are alike. Remind students that self-respect is important, too. In sharing information, students should talk about their own qualities they are proud of.

4. Ask students to name other valuable personal qualities. These qualities might include fairness, integrity, taking responsibilities, trying hard even when things get difficult. Write these responses on the board. Encourage students to define these values and explain why they are important. Ask students to describe situations when these qualities are important.

5. Distribute **Student Handout 1: Words of Wisdom.** Have students interpret the quotations on their own. Then have a class discussion to share the responses. Possible answers are provided in the answer key.

6. Distribute **Student Handout 2: Making Decisions.** Help students understand the decision-making process shown on the handout. Explain that, after coming up with two possible solutions, it helps to consider civic values in making a final decision. Encourage students to also seek advice from people they respect before making a final decision. Review the two situations on the handout. Have students work in groups to complete the handout for each situation. In a class discussion, encourage the groups to compare their outcomes.

ENRICHMENT

1. To foster respect among the students, write the name of each student on a piece of paper. Distribute the papers randomly. Ask students to think about the person whose name is on their paper and write something they respect about the person. Collect all the papers and distribute them to each person whose name is on the paper.

2. Have each student read biographical information about one of the following people: Jimmy Carter, Martin Luther King, Jr., Harriet Tubman, and Jane Addams. Ask students to report how these people demonstrated one or more of these values: fairness, responsibility, respect, and trustworthiness.

Words of Wisdom   Civic Participation

Here are some notable quotations about civic values. Write a few sentences about what these words mean and how they might apply today.

1. "One falsehood spoils a thousand truths."—Ashanti Proverb

_____

_____

2. "No one can make you feel inferior without your consent."—Eleanor Roosevelt

_____

_____

3. "Never grow a wishbone, daughter, where your backbone ought to be."—Clementine Paddleford

_____

_____

4. "Show me a guy who's afraid to look bad, and I'll show you a guy you can beat every time."—Lou Brock

_____

_____

5. "Ask not what your country can do for you—ask what you can do for your country."—John F. Kennedy

_____

_____

6. "A person reveals his character by nothing so clearly as the joke he resents."—Georg Christoph Lichtenberg

_____

_____

7. "A candle loses nothing by lighting another."—Anonymous

_____

_____

Making Decisions   Civic Participation

With your group, choose one of these problems. On another piece of paper, make a chart like the one below. Fill in the boxes as you decide on a solution. As you make your decisions, consider applying civic values, such as loyalty, respect, responsibility, honesty, and fairness.

A. Your friend tells you she had to visit her grandmother in the hospital last night. She didn't have time to do her homework. She asks to copy your homework.

B. You want to buy your mother or father a terrific birthday present. You've only saved a few dollars. In the parking lot of the mall, you find a wallet with $50 in it. There is also identification with the owner's name and address.

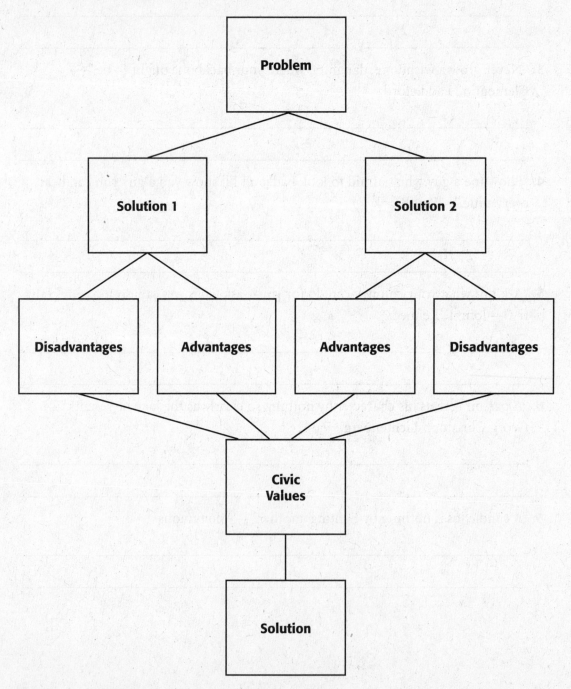

OVERVIEW

The creators of the U.S. Constitution feared a central government with too much power over the people. As a result, they designed three branches of government with both *separation of powers* and *checks and balances.* As students learn how the branches of our government work, they can become responsible participants in the governmental process.

PLANNING
Time Suggested
Two 45-minute class periods

Materials

- Student Handout 1: Separation of Powers

- Student Handout 2: Making a Law

- Reference information for students to locate names of their local representatives to Congress, federal courthouses, and information about the national government.

- Three pieces of butcher paper, markers

Preparation
Reserve time in the school library for students to research the three branches of government (for **Student Handout 1, Part One**). For **Student Handout 1, Part Two,** collect information about local representatives and courts, or find a Web site that students can access.

Suggested Resources
Some helpful resources for **Student Handout 1, Part One** might include a U.S. history textbook, encyclopedia, or a Web site for *Ben's Guide to U.S. Government for Kids* from the U.S. Government Printing Office at http://bensguide.gpo.gov/6-8/government/branches.html.

Group Size
Organize students into three groups, representing the legislative (Congress), executive, and judicial branches.

OBJECTIVES

- Students will learn about the three branches of government and why the creators of the Constitution wanted a separation of powers.

- Students will learn about the organization of the three branches and how their powers overlap.

- Students will research specific information about their government.

- Students will simulate functions of different branches of government.

PROCEDURE

1. **Focus Activity** Ask students to pretend they are delegates at the Constitutional Convention. The colonies have just won independence from Britain. The delegates strongly want to create a government in which no one part of the government, nor any person or group, has too much power. Guide the discussion so that students consider solutions for creating a successful government based on rights, liberty, and representation. Students may propose a model similar to the U. S. government with a separation of powers between legislative, executive, and judicial branches.

2. Distribute Student **Handout 1: Separation of Powers.** Have the groups complete **Part One: Three Branches.** Answers are provided in the answer key.

3. Next, assign each group to be one branch of government. Ask the groups to do research on the powers of that branch. They may use books, encyclopedias, or the Web site listed in the Suggested Resources section. They should write these powers on a piece of butcher paper. Display the completed lists and have the groups talk about how the powers of the branches are separate but overlapping. For example, the legislative branch writes and passes laws; the executive branch can propose laws and can veto laws; the judicial branch can declare laws unconstitutional. Explain that this overlap in responsibilities is called "checks and balances" and was created in the Constitution to limit the power of each branch. Have students complete **Part Two: Your Government.**

5. Have students use resources to find out how a law is made. Discuss the process in class. Distribute **Student Handout 2: Making a Law.** Students should fill out the handout during this process. Have students summarize the legislation in the space available. Remind students that a law can start in the executive or legislative branch. Explain that, in this case, students in the executive branch will start the process by presenting an issue to Congress. Have the class choose a president and vice president from the executive branch. The rest of the executive branch should advise the president and vice president. Members of the executive branch should talk about an issue for which they think a law is needed. You might suggest ideas such as reducing air or water pollution, banning SUVs to conserve oil supplies, or providing government money for all students to attend college for free. Organize the students in the legislative branch into a Senate and a House of Representatives. Each house should discuss the wording of the bill and the specific conditions they want. In their discussions, they should consider the needs of their constituents (people who elect them to office). Then the House of Representatives and Senate should talk together to come up with wording that both houses can pass. Each house must vote on the bill and pass it by a simple majority. When both houses have approved the bill, they should pass it on to the president for approval. The president can sign the bill or veto it. If the bill is vetoed, both houses of Congress can override the veto with a two-thirds vote of each house. Note that if the president neither vetoes nor signs a bill, it becomes law. While the executive and legislative branches are writing the law, the judicial branch should consider whether it might violate any part of the Constitution.

ENRICHMENT

Have students find out what bills are being, or will be, discussed in Congress. Have each student write a letter to a senator or representative to voice an opinion on a bill.

Name _____ Class _____ Date _____

The Branches of Government   Separation of Powers

PART ONE: THREE BRANCHES

Write the words from the Word Bank into the chart. You may use references to find the answers.

House of Representatives   Federal Courts   Vice President

Senate   President   Cabinet

Supreme Court

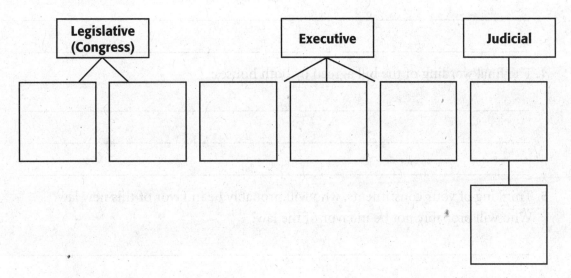

PART TWO: YOUR GOVERNMENT

1. Name the president and vice president of the United States.

_____

2. Name three people in the cabinet and their titles.

_____

3. Name the U.S. senators from your state.

_____

4. How many people in the House of Representatives represent your state? Name the representative from your district.

_____

5. Where is the federal court nearest your home?

_____

6. Name the most recently appointed Supreme Court justice.

_____

Name _____ Class _____ Date _____

The Branches of Government

Making a Law

1. The new law will address the issue of _____

2. The House of Representatives draft of the bill:

_____

_____

3. The Senate draft of the bill:

_____

_____

4. The final wording of the bill agreed by both houses:

_____

_____

_____

5. Thinking of your constituents, who will probably be in favor of this new law? Who will probably not be in favor of the law?

_____

_____

6. What constitutional issues concern the judicial branch? Might any rights be violated by the law?

_____

_____

7. Both houses of Congress should take a roll-call. Each member should call out his/her "yes" or "no" vote. How many members of your group must approve the bill for a simple majority?

_____

8. If the bill passes both houses, pass it on to the president for a signature or a veto. President's action:

_____

9. Do you think government would be better if it did not take so long to make and pass a law? Explain your answer.

_____

_____

Civic Participation

OVERVIEW

Write the following quote on the board: "Leaders build teams and teams build leaders." Discuss the quote briefly with students. Ask students to begin to think about what qualities make a good leader. Knowing these qualities can help a person choose a good leader as well as be a good leader. Tell students that in this lesson they will discuss the qualities of a good leader and hold an election for a class leader.

PLANNING

Time Suggested

Two 45-minute class periods

Materials

- Student Handout 1: Qualities of a Good Leader
- Student Handout 2: Electing a Leader
- Four pieces of poster board, markers
- A small piece of paper for each student (to be used as ballots)
- A shoebox for the ballots

Group Size

Organize students into four groups.

OBJECTIVES

- Students will learn about qualities of good leaders and qualities that hinder good leadership.
- Students will choose between effective and ineffective leadership skills.
- Students will learn about an election process of nominating candidates, speaking in favor of a candidate, and voting.
- Students will conduct an election.

PROCEDURE

1. **Focus Activity** Ask students to think of people—from school, the community, the business world, or government—who are good leaders. List the people's names on the board. Ask students to tell why they think each person is a good leader. Write notes under each person's name. When the chart is complete, ask students to name qualities that are common to these leaders, such as they are hard working or they get results.

2. Discuss the following leadership skills. Ask students to describe a situation in which each skill would be helpful.

   A. Communicator: A good leader can convey ideas in simple ways. She/he listens to other people's suggestions and guides the team instead of pushing his/her ideas on others. A good leader can persuade others.

B. Motivator: A good leader challenges people to accomplish a goal instead of "bossing" people around. A good leader teaches others rather than doing the job for them.

C. Decision Maker: A good leader looks at the facts, considers the consequences, and makes a fair decision. A good leader is decisive, but is also flexible if the facts and consequences change.

D. Team Builder: A good leader encourages people to work together. She/he is honest when things are not working and helps people learn from mistakes. A good leader gives positive comments whenever possible.

2. Distribute **Student Handout 1: Qualities of a Good Leader.** Ask students to work in groups to complete the handout. Then ask each group to pick one of the situations and role-play it for the class. Encourage students to talk about situations in which they experienced a leader with good or poor leadership skills.

3. Explain that the class is going to elect a class leader to accomplish a task with the class. Ask students to pick a project, such as planning a fundraiser, documenting a school event, or planning a party. Ask each group to decide which person from their group they want to nominate as leader. Students should consider the leadership skills they have discussed. Remind students to be tactful in their discussion. They should focus on each other's positive qualities rather than the negative ones.

4. Distribute **Student Handout 2: Electing a Leader.** After students have decided on a candidate, they should write the person's name in Box A. In the box, they should list positive leadership qualities about the person. They can also make notes about the person's successful experiences as a leader or team member.

5. Teams should prepare an election campaign for their candidates. Using their notes on the handout, teams should write a 30-second commercial for each candidate and create a poster. Teams should present their campaigns in front of the class. During the presentation, students should jot notes about the other candidates in boxes B, C, and D.

6. Hold an election to choose a leader. Students should write the name of one candidate on a piece of paper, fold it, and put it in a shoebox. Count the ballots and announce the winner.

7. Have the leader hold a class discussion about accomplishing the task. After plans are made and work assigned, ask students to discuss the leader's skills.

ENRICHMENT

1. Before the election, hold a debate among the four candidates. Assign some students to make up questions to ask each of the candidates, such as "How would you handle a person who doesn't want to work on the project?" Give each candidate 30 seconds to answer each question. Encourage students to discuss the difference among the candidates.

2. Ask students to bring in—if possible—campaign literature from a local or national election. Discuss what leadership qualities the literature emphasizes. Talk about what kind of language and artwork makes persuasive campaign literature. Ask students to discuss anything about the campaign literature that they don't like, that doesn't seem persuasive or true. Ask students why someone would include that information in the literature.

Name _____ Class _____ Date _____

Qualities of a Good Leader   Civic Participation

Read each situation. Tell how team members might react to each of the leader's comments. Check the better thing for the leader to say. Then tell what leadership qualities are shown by your choice.

1. Team member: We can't get the project done by noon tomorrow. It's impossible.

Leader:

_____ **A.** You guys aren't trying hard enough. You're just too slow.
How will team members feel?

_____

_____ **B.** Let's divide up the work. Tell me what job you can do best.
How will team members feel?

_____

What leadership qualities are shown by your choice?

_____

2. Team member: I'd like to operate the video camera, but I'm not sure how to do it.

Leader:

_____ **A.** I'll show you. Try it for a while. Let me know if you have questions.
How will the team member feel?

_____

_____ **B.** Forget it. I know how to operate the camera. I'll do it.
How will the team member feel?

_____

What leadership qualities are shown by your choice?

_____

Qualities of a Good Leader, *continued*   Civic Participation

3. Leader:

_____ **A.** I know you want to have a Halloween Party for the class, but there's so much to do. Let's talk about it some other time.
How will team members feel?

_____

_____ **B.** There's a lot to do if we want to have a Halloween Party. If everyone wants one, let's make it happen.
How will team members feel?

_____

What leadership qualities are shown by your choice?

_____

4. Team member: It looks like the photographs for the project didn't come out.

Leader:

_____ **A.** It's Dana's fault. She insisted on taking the photographs.
How will team members feel?

_____

_____ **B.** Let's figure out what went wrong. I think we have time to try again.
How will team members feel?

_____

What leadership qualities are shown by your choice?

_____

Name _____ Class _____ Date _____

Electing a Leader   Civic Participation

Before you vote for a leader, find out as much as you can about the candidates' skills and experience. Read information, listen to speeches and debates, and ask questions. Take notes in the boxes below. After you make your choice, find a way to work effectively with the leader to accomplish the group's goals.

Name _____	Name _____

Name _____	Name _____

I made my decision because _____

_____

I can help the leader succeed by _____

_____

OVERVIEW

In the United States system of federalism, the power to govern is shared between the national government and the states. Students will examine how and why the writers of the Constitution designated powers to the federal and state governments. Working in groups, students will examine Supreme Court cases in which federal and state laws conflicted. Students will explore these conflicts and form decisions about them.

PLANNING

Time Suggested

Two 45-minute class periods

Materials

- Student Handout 1: Who Has the Power?
- Student Handout 2: Supreme Court Decisions
- Copies of the United States Constitution and Bill of Rights (located in the student textbook)

Suggested Resources

The Supreme Court cases on Student Handout 2 can be found at www.supct.law.cornell.edu/supct/cases/historic/htm or by searching "Supreme Court Historic Decisions."

Group Size

Organize students into groups of 5 to 6 students each.

OBJECTIVES

- Students will create a living situation in which they consider the advantages of pooling resources as well as the need to preserve individual rights.
- Students will learn how the United States system of federalism distributes, shares, and limits powers of the national and state governments.
- Students will examine Supreme Court cases in which state laws have been disputed.

PROCEDURE

1. **Focus Activity** Have students sit in groups. Ask: "How many students share a bedroom at home?" Present the following proposition: "Suppose you were offered a chance to have a much larger bedroom. Let's call it Megaroom. Besides being bigger, it would have more and better things in it." Ask students to name some of the things they would love to have in this room. (These things might include computers, cooking equipment, a large-screen TV.) Encourage students to draw pictures of Megaroom. Then add: "You can have all this, but you will need to share the room with all the other people in your group." Ask: "What might you gain from this arrangement? Would there be disadvantages? What would they be?"

2. Explain that deciding to participate in this room is similar to the 13 original states joining together to create a central government. After the Declaration of Independence, the 13 colonies were like 13 separate countries with their own constitutions. They decided to join together. One important advantage of joining together was the ability to build a stronger military. The military was important for keeping the colonies independent from Britain. A central government also simplified some things, such as printing national money instead of having each state make its own. Nevertheless, many Americans did not want to form a central government, because they feared they would lose their individual freedom and liberties. That is why writing the Constitution and Bill of Rights was such a complicated and important job. Encourage students to talk about Megaroom and the individual rights they would want to keep if they moved into the room. These rights might include the right to stay up as late as they want or the right to have a quiet, dark room after 10 P.M. There will likely be conflicting desires for these individual rights. Allow students to try to persuade each other to agree on a compromise.

3. Explain that all 50 states have their own state governments with three branches similar to the national government. The writers of the Constitution spelled out how state and national governments share powers. This allowed states to deal with their own needs, which might differ because of location, natural resources, and values of the people. It also allowed the states to act together in the federal government to deal with other countries. Since the Civil War, the national government has gotten more involved in how the states treat citizens. For example, although many states allowed segregated schools for African Americans or making people pay a "voting tax," Congress passed amendments to the Constitution to forbid these actions. These amendments protect the civil rights of citizens. Distribute **Handout 1: Who Has the Power?** Discuss the powers listed in the chart. Then have each group of students discuss answers to the questions and report them to the class. Allow students to challenge each other on their answers.

4. Distribute **Student Handout 2: Supreme Court Decisions.** Read each court case and be sure students understand the issues. Then have each group discuss the questions and form opinions. For Case A, refer students to the First and Fourteenth Amendments. For Case B, refer them to the First Amendment. The decisions of the Supreme Court are given in the answer key.

ENRICHMENT

1. Assign students to read and report on the essays known as *The Federalist,* written by James Madison, Alexander Hamilton, and John Jay. These essays supported the Constitution and argued that the nation needed a strong central government. A group called the Anti-Federalists opposed this opinion. They insisted that the Constitution needed a Bill of Rights to protect individual freedoms. Divide the class into two teams: the Federalists and Anti-Federalists and have them debate their opinions.

2. Have students write a constitution for the Megaroom. It should have a preamble and articles that describe the common property in the room and the rights and responsibilities of the individuals.

3. Have students create a poster with the name of their state's governor, the governor's term of office, qualifications (age, length of residency, citizenship), and responsibilities. They should add news articles about the governor.

Who Has the Power?   Civic Participation

National Government	Shared Powers	State Government
• Print money • Declare war • Build an army and navy • Make treaties with other countries • Oversee trade between states • Set up post offices	• Collect taxes • Build roads • Set up courts • Enforce laws • Borrow money • Provide for the general welfare	• Conduct elections • Issue licenses (driver's, hunting, marriage, etc.) • Set up local governments • Ratify amendments • Oversee the safety and welfare of the people within the state

1. Why do you think the national government controls the power to print money?

_____

_____

_____

2. Why do you think state governments set the age for getting a driver's license?

_____

_____

_____

3. When the Thirteenth Amendment was passed in 1865, the national government took away the right of states to decide if slavery would be legal in the state. Why do you think a national law was passed about this?

_____

_____

_____

4. States, not the national government, make laws about the death penalty for certain crimes. Do you think states should have this power? Why or why not?

_____

_____

_____

Supreme Court Decisions   Civic Participation

Each paragraph below tells about a Supreme Court case. In each case, citizens argued that a state law violated a part of the Constitution. Read about each case and talk about it with your group. Answer the questions. Support your decisions.

A. Arkansas had a law that required public school teachers to fill out and sign a form every year. The teachers had to list every organization to which they belonged or regularly contributed within the preceding five years. A group of teachers refused to fill out this form. Those teachers lost their jobs. The teachers started a lawsuit complaining that the state did not respect their freedom of association. [*Shelton* v. *Tucker* (1960)]

1. Why might the state have wanted the list of associations?

_____

2. Why might the teachers have refused to fill out the form?

_____

3. What decision do you think the Supreme Court should have made?

_____

B. Nebraska's state legislature began each session with a prayer. A chaplain was paid by the state to lead this prayer. A member of the legislature started a lawsuit saying that this practice violated the First Amendment. [*Marsh* v. *Chambers* (1983)]

1. What does the First Amendment say about religion?

_____

2. Why did the member of the legislature start a lawsuit?

_____

3. What decision do you think the Supreme Court should have made?

_____

OVERVIEW

One of our nation's most important institutions is its judicial system. The judicial system interprets laws and protects the rights of citizens. Students will learn about the trial process and conduct a mock trial for a civil case. The judicial system has many levels, and the process cannot be thoroughly covered in this lesson. The purpose of the lesson is to familiarize students with the concept and goals of a civil trial.

PLANNING

Time Suggested

Three to four 45-minute class periods

Materials

- Copies of the Bill of Rights (located in the student textbook)
- Student Handout 1: Preparing for Trial
- Student Handout 2: The Trial

Group Size

Organize students into four groups.

OBJECTIVES

- Students will learn how the Bill of Rights protects citizens in the judicial system.
- Students will learn vocabulary terms and apply them to describe a civil lawsuit.
- Students will prepare for a mock trial by discussing the details of a civil case.
- Students will conduct a mock trial.

PROCEDURE

1. **Focus Activity** You may want to invite a local attorney—especially one who practices civil law rather than criminal law—to help students through this first step. Most courtroom television dramas are about criminal trials, and even stations such as Court TV may focus on criminal trials. Civil trials and civil procedure are a little different. An attorney as a guide would be useful. Let students share what they know about the judicial trial process. Ask each student to say any fact he or she knows about trials. Students may have a number of ideas gleaned from watching television. These ideas may include, "The accused person is called the defendant;" "There is a jury;" "A person is presumed innocent until proven guilty." Continue eliciting facts until no one can think of any more.

2. Explain that United States citizens have unique protections that do not exist in every country. Laws give protections to people accused of crimes, such as the right to a speedy public trial with an impartial jury, the right to hear and question all witnesses against them, and the protection against cruel and unusual punishment. Distribute copies of the Bill of Rights. Assign groups of students to read the Fifth, Sixth, Seventh, and Eighth Amendments. Have the students report to the class on how the amendment protects citizens' rights. Explain that the Fifth, Sixth, and Eighth, amendments relate to criminal cases, when someone is accused of committing a crime. Many cases are civil cases, when there is a disagreement between people or groups.

3. Distribute **Student Handout 1: Preparing for Trial.** Have student use dictionaries to define the words in Part One: Trial Terms. Discuss the definitions to be sure students understand them. Then read the paragraph in Part Two: The Case. Tell students to use the words from Part One to complete the sentences in Part Two. Answers are in the answer key.

4. Ask probing questions about the case of *Ed Grant* v. *Harrington Hardware Manufacturers.* For example: Is Ed Grant at all responsible for the accident? Could the rung of the ladder have broken for some other reason than poor manufacturing? What evidence should be presented in the trial? What role can the neighbor and the mail carrier play in the trial? Can anyone else support either side?

5. Distribute **Student Handout 2: The Trial.** Have students work in groups to complete the handout. Then explain the roles in the mock trial:

- The **plaintiff** and **plaintiff's attorney** try to prove that the defendant is responsible for the plaintiff's losses. The plaintiff's attorney puts the plaintiff and the plaintiff's witnesses on the stand, under oath, and asks them questions designed to present the facts in the light most favorable to the plaintiff.

- The **defendant** and **defendant's attorney** try to show that they are not to blame. The defendant's attorney puts the defendant and the defendant's witnesses on the stand to testify and to present the facts in the light most favorable to the defendant. The defendant may try to show what other circumstances might have been responsible for the damages.

- **Witnesses,** some for each side, tell what they saw, knew, or did. Expert witnesses can offer opinions (most ordinary witnesses cannot). The attorney for the other side can question a party's witnesses to challenge their reliability. The goal is to show that the witness may be mistaken, may not be believable, may have misunderstood something, or has a faulty memory. For example, the attorney might try to prove that the witnesses did not actually see the entire incident.

- The **court reporter** takes notes of all the trial proceedings.

- The **judge** instructs the members of the jury before they start their deliberations.

- The **jury** decides in favor of the plaintiff or the defendant and determines the amount of the award, if any, to the plaintiff.

6. Ask for volunteers to role-play these people: Ed Grant (the plaintiff), Ed Grant's attorney, a representative of Harrington Hardware Manufacturers (the defendant), Harrington Hardware's attorney, Patti Brown, Harry Valdez, the court reporter, and the judge. The rest of the class should be on the jury. Assign a jury foreperson who will organize the jury deliberation and report the jury's verdict. Before the trial begins, the plaintiff or defendant can pull people from the jury to play the role of additional witnesses or experts, such as doctors.

Allow at least one 45-minute session to hold the mock trial. Afterward, encourage students to talk about the outcome of the trial.

ENRICHMENT

1. Have students make up another case and write a paragraph about it using the terms from Student Handout 1. Let them discuss one of these cases or hold another mock trial.

2. Have students use an encyclopedia, other reference books, or the Internet to learn about the Supreme Court case of *Miranda* v. *Arizona*. Ask students to report on how this case affected the rights of the accused in a criminal case.

Preparing for Trial

Civic Participation

PART ONE: TRIAL TERMS

Use a dictionary to write short definitions for these words.

1. plaintiff _____

2. defendant _____

3. attorney _____

4. judge _____

5. jury _____

6. witness _____

PART TWO: THE CASE

On June 23, Ed Grant noticed that the weather vane from his roof had been blown into a tall tree in his yard. Ed had just bought a new ladder made by Harrington Hardware Manufacturers. Ed climbed the ladder and was reaching for the weather vane when the rung of the ladder broke, and Ed fell to the ground. Patti Brown, the mail carrier, saw Ed fall and rushed to help. Harry Valdez, a neighbor, also saw the accident. For the next three months, Ed had thousands of dollars in medical bills and was unable to work at his restaurant. He decided to sue Harrington Hardware Manufacturers for the money he lost.

3. In this case, Ed Grant is the _____.

4. Harrington Hardware Manufacturers is the _____.

5. Patti Brown and Harry Valdez are _____.

6. In many civil cases, the parties settle out of court, but Harry and his _____ have decided they want a trial.

7. Many small civil trials are decided by a _____, but Harry wants it decided by a _____ of 12 people.

The Trial   Civic Participation

1. What is the plaintiff's complaint?

_____

2. What facts might the defendant offer to show they were not responsible?

_____

3. Who are the witnesses?

_____

4. Write two questions that the plaintiff's attorney might ask the witnesses—plaintiff's witnesses or defendant's witnesses—to support Ed Grant's side.

_____

_____

5. Write two questions that the defendant's attorney might ask witnesses—plaintiff's witnesses or defendant's witnesses—to support the defendant's arguments.

_____

_____

6. Write a closing statement by the plaintiff's attorney to persuade the jury to Ed Grant's side.

_____

_____

7. Write a closing statement by the defendant's attorney to persuade the jury to Harrington Hardware Manufacturer's side.

_____

_____

8. If you were on the jury, what decision would you make? Why?

_____

_____

OVERVIEW

United States citizens each enjoy individual rights and freedoms, but society as a whole works because of a sense of community. In this lesson, students will consider how people work together in and for a community. They will plan a community project and examine situations in which citizens might act for the common welfare even when it conflicts with some individuals' needs.

PLANNING

Time Suggested

Two 45-minute class periods
Additional time outside of class may be needed to conduct the volunteer projects.

Materials

- a timer
- Student Handout 1: A Community Project
- Student Handout 2: The Common Welfare

Group Size

For the Focus Activity, organize students into two groups. For the other activities, organize students into groups of 4 to 6 students.

OBJECTIVES

- Students will discuss special events and places in the community and identify how citizens help make these events and places possible.
- Students will learn how volunteers can make a community better. Then they will design their own volunteer projects.
- Students will learn about common welfare and analyze situation when common welfare conflicts with individual interests.
- Students will discuss alternative solutions to community problems.

PROCEDURE

1. **Focus Activity** Play a picture-drawing game. Organize the class into two teams. Have one person from Team A pick an event or place in the community and start to draw the place or event on the board. Set a timer or a stopwatch and stop it when someone from Team A guesses the place or event. Repeat the procedure for Team B. Have all the players from each team take turns. Tally all the times. The team with the shortest total guessing time wins.

2. Start a discussion on places and events in the community of which the students are proud. Ask: "How do citizens help make the event or place possible? Which people are paid employees? Which are volunteers? What would happen if the citizens did not participate?" Help students understand that a successful community needs citizens who give their time, often as volunteers.

3. Distribute **Student Handout 1: A Community Project.** Organize the class into groups of 4 to 6 students. Ask students to think of ways they could volunteer their time and energy to help the community. Explain that "community" does not have to mean "neighborhood." It could refer to a school community, a neighborhood or town, a region, or the nation, as long as there is a spirit of working together for a common goal. You might suggest ideas such as cooking a senior citizens' lunch at a church; cleaning up a park or playground; starting a recycling drive; or collecting and donating used sports equipment to needy children. Students should use the handout to plan the project in class. If you think the projects are feasible, arrange for students to carry them out. Be sure students check with adults who need to approve those projects and are available to supervise.

4. Distribute **Student Handout 2: The Common Welfare.** Ask students to guess what is meant by "the common welfare." Explain that a government spends taxpayers' money and tries to find solutions that help as many citizens as possible. Sometimes decisions that are best for the common welfare are not best for some individuals. For example, the United States government has imposed security checkpoints for luggage and passengers at airports. These checkpoints often create long lines and inconvenience travelers. However, the procedures are for the common welfare: the safety of everyone on the plane and, in a larger view, the security of the nation.

5. When students have completed the handout, discuss the responses. Encourage students to come up with alternative solutions to the problems.

6. Ask students to list ways in which community organizations made up mostly of volunteers can help or even replace some government programs. Some programs might include health clinics in some neighborhoods and food kitchens and shelters for poor people. Ask students also to list some things that the government probably must do because the task is too large for volunteers. Such programs might include paying for highway and bridge construction and providing armed forces.

ENRICHMENT

1. Have students create a promotional booklet for their community. Some students should take photographs and draw pictures of several places in their community. Others should write descriptions. Collate the information into a booklet and display it at the library.

2. Ask students to look through newspapers and magazines to find articles about topics that relate to the common welfare. Encourage students to voice their opinions about the issues.

Name _____ Class _____ Date _____

A Community Project   Civic Participation

Discuss with your group some projects that might let you make a difference in your community. Have the group select one project.

1. Describe the project that your group can do for the community.

_____

_____

_____

_____

2. Who would be helped by this project?

_____

_____

3. List the adults you would need to talk to for approval of this idea.

_____

_____

4. When would you begin this project?

_____

5. How much time do you need to prepare? _____

6. How long will the project take? _____

Assign responsibilities to the group:

Name(s)   **Task**

_____ Contact the place or organization you want
                         to help.

_____ Contact the adults who need to approve
                         and supervise the plan.

_____ Buy or collect supplies.

_____ Make flyers and signs, and send a press
                         release to the local newspaper.

_____ Participate at the project site.

The Common Welfare

Civic Participation

Sometimes people should give up their own interests for the common welfare. Sometimes they shouldn't. It's a personal decision. Talk about such situations with your group. Answer the questions.

1. School enrollment has grown in the last five years. There is a shortage of classrooms. If the government raises property taxes on every resident by an average of $200 a year, an addition can be built onto the school. The residents must vote for this plan. Many residents don't have children in the school and feel they will not benefit from the school addition.

A. Would the school addition be for the common welfare? Explain.

_____

_____

B. If you were a resident without children in school, how would you vote? Explain.

_____

_____

2. XYZ factory is struggling to stay in business. Now it might become even more expensive to run. Many people object to air pollution caused by the factory. Those people want to pass a law prohibiting the factory from burning waste materials. XYZ and similar nearby factories might have to close. Many people would lose their jobs.

A. Would the air pollution law be for the common welfare? Explain.

_____

_____

B. Would you be in favor of the law? Explain.

_____

_____

3. Can you think of circumstances in which accepting something negative might actually have a positive benefit? For example, if the air around the factories was already polluted and burning the wastes did not increase the pollution beyond a certain point, would it be worth it to accept the extra pollution in order to save jobs? What might that "certain point" be? Would time be a factor in your decision? Work with your classmates to see if you can solve this problem.

OVERVIEW

Good citizens are watchful of ways that the community can improve. They take action to make positive changes. In this lesson, students will identify a problem in the community, study it, and propose a public policy to deal with the problem. Then they will create a plan of action to gather support and take their proposal to a governing body.

PLANNING
Time Suggested

Three 45-minute class periods
Additional time may be needed to talk to people in the community.

Materials

- Local newspapers with articles about community issues and problems
- Student Handout 1: The Problem
- Student Handout 2: The Plan

Preparation

- Collect local newspapers articles about issues that students might want to change. Select some "Letters to the editor" that talk about local problems or issues.

Group Size

Organize students into 4–6 groups.

OBJECTIVES

- Students will identify an issue or problem in their community.
- Students will research if and how the problem is being addressed.
- Students will create a policy that changes or replaces an existing policy.
- Students will develop an action plan to get their proposal accepted by authorities.

PROCEDURE

1. **Focus Activity** Begin a conversation about change. Ask students how they would go about making a change in the following situations:

   - They put on a red sweatshirt in the morning and then decide they wanted to wear a brown sweatshirt. (They could easily make the change.)
   - They think the classroom desks should be arranged in groups instead of in rows. (They could make the suggestion to the teacher and try to get the support of classmates.)
   - They feel school starts too early and want the schedule changed to start later. (This type of change requires research, planning, and getting support. Suggestions include: Talk about who is responsible for changing the school schedule. Discuss who might be affected and

what the consequences are of a later start time. Things such as after-school activities or teacher contracts need to be considered. Ask if there are any laws that dictate how many hours students must be in school.)

2. Distribute **Student Handout 1: The Problem.** Explain that each group must agree on a problem or issue that group members believe needs changing in the community. They can look through newspapers to get ideas. In addition, you could name some topics for them to brainstorm, such as parks, playgrounds, recreational areas, the business district, schools, the library, traffic, animals, health, and safety. For the questions in Part Two, encourage students to read articles, ask their parents, and interview people in authority. Help students understand the importance of gathering facts and knowing how this problem has been handled in the past. As students start to find answers to Part Two, they may decide to change or reword the problem in Part One. Allow students to make changes in Part One as long as they complete Part Two about the problem.

3. Distribute **Student Handout 2: The Plan.** It is important to stress that a good plan must be realistic and supported by facts and testimony. Students may want to talk to people in other towns or schools who have dealt with a similar problem. Allow at least one class period for students to complete Part One: Writing a Policy. Students should draft the policy on another piece of paper before finalizing it. To complete the details in Items 1 and 2, students might need to talk to people and use resources outside of the classroom.

4. Ask students to complete Part Two: Making an Action Plan. Review the details of the plan to be sure students have been thorough and practical. Then have students begin putting their plan into action. They can write letters to the editor of the newspaper and to other groups who might support them. They can create posters and flyers to circulate in the community. They might hold an information session at the school or library to present their views and listen to opposition. Then they can contact the approval group and make an appointment to discuss the plan.

ENRICHMENT

1. Have students find out how community policies have been changed in the past. If there is a new playground or a new school policy, students should find out who influenced the change and how long the process took. They should report their findings to the class.

2. Encourage students to read about the temperance movement that started in the 1800s and the period of Prohibition (1920-1933). The temperance movement started with a group of people who believed alcohol caused most of the nation's social problems. The Eighteenth Amendment started Prohibition, making the sale of alcohol illegal in the United States. As crime rose during Prohibition, people decided that the movement was not succeeding. The 21st Amendment repealed the Prohibition policy.

The Problem   Civic Participation

PART ONE: IDENTIFYING THE PROBLEM

1. Name a problem or issue in your community that you would like to change.

_____

2. Why is it a problem?

_____

_____

3. Who is affected by the problem? Does it affect the whole community or just a small group?

_____

_____

PART TWO: EXAMINING SOLUTIONS

1. What individuals, groups, or branch of government is responsible for this problem?

_____

_____

2. Right now, is anything happening to try to deal with the problem? What?

_____

_____

3. What do you think about the current solution or idea for the solution? What are its strengths?

_____

_____

4. What, if any, are weaknesses of the proposed solution?

_____

_____

5. To whom can you talk to learn more about this problem and possible solutions?

_____

_____

The Plan   Civic Participation

PART ONE: WRITING A POLICY

1. Write a policy to solve the problem.

_____

_____

2. What individuals or group would be responsible for overseeing the change? Why?

_____

3. How much would your policy cost? Who would pay this cost? Is it more or less than the cost of the current policy?

_____

_____

PART TWO: MAKING AN ACTION PLAN

Describe how you will try to get your plan accepted. Write target dates for accomplishing each step.

Date: _____ **1.** What groups or individuals will support your plan? How will you contact them and ask for their support?

_____

_____

Date: _____ **2.** What groups or individuals will likely oppose your plan? How can you respond to their concerns?

_____

_____

Date: _____ **3.** How can you get support from the general public?

_____

_____

Date: _____ **4.** How will you contact everyone who must approve the policy change? How will you present your plan?

_____

_____